Quick and H...
30 Minute Recipes
for Busy People

Easy Prep Kitchen Meals
for a Balanced Lifestyle

Emily Harper

Quick and Healthy 30 Minute Recipes for Busy People

Easy Prep Kitchen Meals for a Balanced Lifestyle

By Emily Harper

Note to Readers: This book is designed to provide delicious, quick, and healthy recipe ideas for busy individuals. While we've made every effort to ensure the accuracy and safety of the information presented, please keep the following in mind:

- The recipes and information are for inspirational and educational purposes only. They are not intended to replace professional medical or nutritional advice.
- Before making significant changes to your diet or lifestyle, we recommend consulting with a healthcare professional or registered dietitian, especially if you have any health concerns or dietary restrictions.
- The nutritional information provided is an estimate based on standard ingredients and serving sizes. Actual values may vary depending on specific brands and quantities used.
- If you have food allergies or sensitivities, please carefully check the ingredients list for each recipe. Some recipes may contain common allergens such as nuts, dairy, eggs, or wheat.
- While we've taken great care in developing these recipes, the author and publisher cannot be held responsible for any adverse reactions or consequences resulting from the use of information in this book.

We hope you enjoy exploring these quick and healthy recipes and find them helpful in your journey towards a balanced lifestyle!

Table of Contents

Introduction

Welcome to "Quick and Healthy 30 Minute Recipes for Busy People"! I am glad you've joined us on this journey into the world of delicious, healthy, and quick cooking. This book is designed for those who strive to eat right but are not ready to spend hours preparing food. In our modern rhythm of life, it often seems that there is simply no time for wholesome, balanced meals. But I am here to prove to you that with the right recipes and approach, healthy eating can be quick and easy.

Every morning when I start my day, I think about how important it is to fuel my body with the energy needed to accomplish all daily tasks. I know that many of you, like me, face a lack of time, especially in the morning. That is why I have included many simple and delicious breakfast recipes in this book to help you start your day with proper nutrition. Imagine how nice it is to wake up knowing that you can quickly prepare something tasty and healthy that will give you energy for the whole day.

Breakfasts are just the beginning. Throughout the day, we all need to find time for lunches and dinners that not only satiate but also benefit our bodies. In this book, you will find a variety of recipes that cater to all taste preferences and dietary needs. Whether it's a light chicken salad or a hearty salmon dish, you will find recipes here that are easy to prepare without compromising on taste or quality.

I have paid special attention to snacks and desserts. Often, it is in these categories that we make the most unhealthy choices. But with the right recipes, you can enjoy delicious snacks and sweets without guilt. In this book, you will find recipes that satisfy your sweet tooth while remaining healthy and easy to prepare.

In addition to quick and healthy meals, I also have extensive experience in specialized diets such as the anti-inflammatory diet, keto diet, and vegetarian cuisine. These diets are known for their health benefits, and I will share my expertise in these areas through future books.

In addition to recipes, I want to share with you several important tips and tricks that I have learned over the years in the kitchen. You will learn how to optimize the cooking process to save time, how to store products properly so that they stay fresh longer, and how to choose ingredients that provide the maximum benefit to your health.

One of the main principles I follow when creating recipes is the use of accessible and simple ingredients. I believe that tasty and healthy dishes do not have to be complicated or expensive. It is important to be able to use what you already have in your kitchen and turn it into masterpieces.

Another important aspect is the flexibility of the recipes. We are all different, and our tastes and preferences can vary greatly. Therefore, many of the recipes in this book can be adapted to your personal preferences.

I hope this book becomes your trusted assistant in the kitchen, a source of inspiration, and an indispensable guide in the world of healthy and quick cooking. I believe that each of us is capable of cooking delicious and healthy food, even if we have very little time. Let "Quick and Healthy 30 Minute Recipes for Busy People" be your secret weapon in the fight for healthy eating and well-being.

Thank you for choosing this book. I am confident that it will help you explore new horizons in cooking and make your daily diet more varied and healthy. Let's embark on this exciting journey to health and the enjoyment of food together!

Best wishes,
Emily Harper

About the Author

Emily Harper is a professional chef and passionate culinary enthusiast who has dedicated her life to creating delicious and healthy recipes. Her culinary journey began in the family kitchen, where she drew inspiration from her grandmother, a master of home cooking. Emily believes that healthy eating should be accessible to everyone, even the busiest individuals.

Over the years, she has developed numerous recipes that help people cook quickly and effortlessly. Collaborating with several renowned restaurants and culinary schools, Emily has gained invaluable experience and knowledge. Her unique approach to cooking, based on using fresh and simple ingredients, has resonated with many health-conscious individuals.

Emily is also well-versed in specialized diets such as the anti-inflammatory diet, keto diet, and vegetarian cuisine. She understands the importance of these dietary approaches for health and well-being and plans to share her expertise in these areas through her future books.

Regular participation in culinary festivals and masterclasses allows her to share her knowledge and inspire others to create their own culinary masterpieces. Her goal is to show that even with limited time, one can prepare delicious and nutritious meals. Emily believes that each day is an opportunity for culinary experiments and enjoying good food. In her free time, she loves to travel, discovering new culinary traditions and dishes from various cultures.

In addition to her professional activities, Emily conducts online courses and webinars, teaching people the basics of healthy eating and quick recipes. These events are highly popular and attract thousands of participants from around the world. Emily aims to show that anyone can learn to cook delicious and healthy meals, regardless of their culinary skills. She also engages in charity work, conducting culinary masterclasses for children and teenagers, teaching them the basics of healthy eating and culinary art. Emily believes that instilling healthy eating habits from an early age helps form lifelong healthy habits.

Introduction to Quick and Delicious Breakfasts

Good morning, busy go-getters! Welcome to the most important chapter of your day – breakfast. In our fast-paced world, it often seems like there's no time for a proper morning meal. But we're here to prove that a delicious, nutritious breakfast can be quick and easy.

Why is breakfast so crucial? It's not just about satisfying your growling stomach; it's about fueling your body and mind for the day ahead. A good breakfast jumpstarts your metabolism, helps control weight, and improves concentration. Regular breakfast eaters often report better heart health, more stable blood sugar levels, and even improved mood!

In this chapter, you'll discover a variety of speedy breakfast recipes that can be whipped up in minutes. From nutrient-packed smoothies to hearty breakfast bowls, there's something here for every taste bud and schedule. We've crafted these recipes to be not just quick, but also balanced, incorporating proteins, complex carbohydrates, and healthy fats to keep you energized and satisfied until lunch.

Quick Tips for Breakfast Success:

1. Plan Ahead: Take some time on the weekend to plan your weekday breakfasts. This small step can save you from morning chaos and unhealthy choices.
2. Prep Your Ingredients: Chop fruits and veggies, hard-boil eggs, or portion out cereals in advance. This can significantly cut down your morning prep time.
3. Embrace Your Freezer: Frozen fruits are perfect for smoothies, and portion-sized frozen breakfast burritos can be quickly reheated in the microwave.
4. Invest in Time-Saving Tools: A good blender, toaster, or egg cooker can become your best friend in quick breakfast preparation.
5. Don't Fear Repetition: If you enjoy a particular breakfast, don't hesitate to have it multiple days in a row. It saves time on decision-making and preparation.

6. Master the Art of Multitasking: While your toast is browning, you can be slicing avocados or frying an egg. Efficient multitasking can cut your prep time in half!
7. Keep a Well-Stocked Pantry: Ensure you always have breakfast essentials on hand. This might include whole grain bread, eggs, Greek yogurt, nuts, and your favorite fruits.
8. Discover Overnight Recipes: Overnight oats or chia puddings can be prepared the night before, giving you a grab-and-go option in the morning.
9. Make Breakfast Portable: Many of our recipes can be easily packed to eat on your commute or at your desk. Invest in some good food containers for mess-free transport.
10. Stay Hydrated: Don't forget to start your day with a glass of water. It can boost your metabolism and help you feel more alert.

Remember, the recipes in this chapter are more than just instructions – they're your secret weapons for starting the day right. Each one has been carefully crafted and tested to ensure it meets our strict criteria: quick to make, delicious to eat, and nourishing for your body.

As you flip through these pages, you'll find that eating a good breakfast doesn't have to mean setting your alarm an hour earlier. With a little preparation and our foolproof recipes, you can enjoy restaurant-quality breakfasts in the comfort of your home, in less time than it takes to wait in line at a café.

So, whether you're a busy professional, a parent getting kids ready for school, or someone who just values those extra minutes of sleep, this chapter is for you. Get ready to transform your mornings and start your days with meals that are as nutritious as they are delicious.

Green Tea Smoothie with Avocado and Spinach

Ingredients:
- 1 ripe avocado
- 1 banana
- 1 cup fresh spinach leaves
- 1 tbsp matcha green tea powder
- 1 cup almond milk (or any preferred milk)
- 1 tbsp honey or agave syrup (optional)
- Ice cubes (optional)

Instructions:
1. Peel and pit the avocado, then cut it into chunks.
2. Peel the banana and break it into pieces.
3. In a blender, combine the avocado, banana, spinach, matcha powder, and almond milk.
4. Blend until smooth and creamy. Add ice cubes if desired.
5. Taste and add honey or agave syrup if preferred.
6. Pour the smoothie into glasses and serve immediately.

Prep time: 5 minutes. Total time: 5 minutes. Serves: 2

Total Nutrition (per serving): Calories: 356; Protein: 6.5g; Carbs: 59.2g; Fat: 24.9g.

Description: This vibrant and nutritious smoothie is perfect for a quick, healthy breakfast or snack. Avocado provides healthy fats, spinach adds greens, and matcha offers a gentle caffeine boost. Packed with vitamins and antioxidants, this smoothie keeps you energized throughout the day.

Tips:
- For extra protein, add a scoop of your favorite protein powder.
- Use frozen banana pieces for a thicker, colder smoothie.
- Leftover smoothie can be stored in an airtight container in the refrigerator for up to 24 hours.

Banana Cinnamon Oatmeal Pancakes

Ingredients:

- 1 ripe banana
- 1 large egg
- 1 cup oat flour (or 1 cup rolled oats, blended)
- 1/2 tsp each: cinnamon, baking powder
- Pinch of salt
- 1/4 cup milk (if needed)
- 1 tbsp coconut oil for cooking

Instructions:

1. If using oats, blend into flour consistency.
2. In a blender, combine banana, egg, oat flour, cinnamon, baking powder, and salt. Blend until smooth. Add milk if needed for a pourable consistency.
3. Heat coconut oil in a non-stick pan over medium heat.
4. Pour 1/4 cup of batter for each pancake. Cook for 2-3 minutes per side until golden brown.
5. Serve warm with maple syrup, honey, or fresh berries if desired.

Prep time: 5 minutes. Cook time: 10 minutes. Total time: 15 minutes. Serves: 2

Total Nutrition (per serving): Calories: 393; Protein: 15.4g; Carbs: 62.5g; Fat: 11.3g.

Description: These fluffy banana cinnamon oatmeal pancakes are a perfect quick and healthy breakfast. The banana adds natural sweetness, reducing the need for added sugar. Oat flour provides fiber and sustained energy. The warm notes of cinnamon create a cozy morning treat.

Tips:

- Use store-bought oat flour for smoother batter.
- Add nuts/chocolate chips for texture.
- Freeze extras and reheat for quick meals.

Spinach and Feta Egg Muffins

Ingredients:
- 6 large eggs
- 1/2 cup milk
- 1 cup fresh spinach, chopped
- 1/2 cup crumbled feta cheese
- 1/4 cup sun-dried tomatoes, chopped
- 1/4 tsp garlic powder
- Salt and pepper to taste
- Cooking spray

Instructions:
1. Preheat oven to 350°F (175°C). Grease a 6-cup muffin tin with cooking spray.
2. In a large bowl, whisk together eggs and milk until well combined.
3. Stir in spinach, feta cheese, sun-dried tomatoes, garlic powder, salt, and pepper.
4. Divide the mixture evenly among the prepared muffin cups.
5. Bake for 20-22 minutes, or until the egg muffins are set and lightly golden on top.
6. Let cool in the tin for 5 minutes before removing and serving.

Prep time: 8 minutes. Cook time: 22 minutes. Total time: 30 minutes. Serves: 3 (2 muffins per serving)

Total Nutrition (per serving): Calories: 347; Protein: 25g; Carbs: 7.5g; Fat: 24.6g.

Description: These spinach and feta egg muffins are a delicious and convenient breakfast option for busy mornings. Packed with protein and vegetables, they offer a satisfying and nutritious start to your day. They're perfect for meal prep – make a batch on Sunday for easy grab-and-go breakfasts all week.

Tips:
- Customize with your favorite vegetables or cheeses.
- Store in airtight container in fridge up to 4 days.
- To reheat, microwave for 30 seconds or until warm.

Honeyed Ricotta Toast with Figs and Pistachios

Ingredients:
- 2 slices of rustic bread
- 1/2 cup ricotta cheese
- 2 tbsp honey, divided
- 2-3 fresh figs, sliced
- 2 tbsp chopped pistachios
- Pinch of sea salt
- Fresh thyme leaves for garnish (optional)

Instructions:
1. Toast bread until golden brown. Mix ricotta with 1 tbsp honey.
2. Spread honeyed ricotta on toast. Top with sliced figs.
3. Drizzle remaining honey over figs. Add pistachios and sea salt.
4. Garnish with thyme if using.

Prep time: 5 minutes. Cook time: 2 minutes. Total time: 7 minutes. Serves: 2

Total Nutrition (per serving): Calories: 314; Protein: 11.2g; Carbs: 43.2g; Fat: 12.3g.

Description: This honeyed ricotta toast with figs and pistachios is a gourmet breakfast that's surprisingly quick to prepare. The creamy ricotta, sweetened with honey, provides a luxurious base for the fresh, succulent figs. Chopped pistachios add a delightful crunch, while a sprinkle of sea salt enhances all the flavors.

Tips:
- If fresh figs are unavailable, use dried figs or seasonal fruit like peaches or berries.
- For a dairy-free version, use almond ricotta or mashed avocado.
- Leftover honeyed ricotta can be stored in the refrigerator for up to 3 days.

Breakfast Burrito with Scrambled Eggs and Avocado

Ingredients:
- 2 large eggs
- 1 tbsp milk
- Salt and pepper to taste
- 1 tsp butter or olive oil
- 1 large flour tortilla
- 1/4 cup shredded cheddar cheese
- 1/2 ripe avocado, sliced
- Optional: 2 tbsp salsa, hot sauce, or sour cream

Instructions:
1. Whisk eggs, milk, salt, and pepper in a bowl. Heat butter/oil in a non-stick skillet over medium heat.
2. Pour egg mixture into skillet, stirring gently until just set, about 2-3 minutes.
3. Meanwhile, warm tortilla in microwave (10-15 seconds) or in a dry skillet (30 seconds per side).
4. Place scrambled eggs in tortilla center; top with cheese and avocado slices.
5. Add optional toppings. Fold sides of tortilla over filling, then tightly roll into a burrito.

Prep time: 3 minutes. Cook time: 5 minutes. Total time: 8 minutes. Serves: 1

Total Nutrition (per serving): Calories: 530; Protein: 26.5g; Carbs: 36g; Fat: 29g.

Description: A quick, customizable breakfast burrito with scrambled eggs, avocado, and cheese. Perfect for busy mornings and easy to eat on-the-go.

Tips:
- Add cooked bacon, ham, or beans for extra protein.
- Use scrambled tofu for a vegetarian option.
- Prep ingredients the night before for quicker assembly.

Cheesy Bacon and Egg Breakfast Sandwich

Ingredients:
- 1 large egg
- 1 English muffin, split and toasted
- 1 slice of cheddar cheese
- 2 slices of cooked bacon
- Salt and pepper to taste
- Optional: sliced avocado, hot sauce, or fresh spinach

Instructions:
1. Heat a small non-stick skillet over medium heat. Crack the egg into the skillet and cook for about 2-3 minutes, or until the white is set but the yolk is still runny.
2. Place the cheese slice on one half of the toasted English muffin. Top with the cooked bacon slices.
3. Carefully place the fried egg on top of the bacon. If desired, add sliced avocado, hot sauce, or fresh spinach for extra flavor and nutrition.
4. Top the sandwich with the other half of the toasted English muffin.
5. Serve the breakfast sandwich immediately while it's still warm and the cheese is melted.

Prep time: 3 minutes. Cook time: 5 minutes. Total time: 8 minutes. Serves: 1

Total Nutrition (per serving): Calories: 393; Protein: 24g; Carbs: 27g; Fat: 21g.

Description: This cheesy bacon and egg breakfast sandwich is a mouthwatering combination of savory flavors and textures that will make your taste buds sing. The crispy, toasted English muffin, melted cheddar cheese, smoky bacon, and a perfectly fried egg with a runny yolk create an irresistible breakfast favorite. Easily customizable with your favorite toppings, this sandwich is perfect for busy mornings when you need a satisfying and indulgent breakfast.

Tropical Sunrise Smoothie Bowl

Ingredients:
- 2 cups frozen fruit (such as mango, pineapple, strawberries, or a mix)
- 1 ripe banana
- 1/2 cup coconut milk (or milk of choice)
- 1/2 cup plain Greek yogurt
- Optional toppings: sliced fruit, shredded coconut, chia seeds, granola

Instructions:
1. Blend Smoothie:
   - In a blender, combine the frozen mango, pineapple, banana, coconut milk, and Greek yogurt.
   - Blend on high speed until smooth and creamy, about 1-2 minutes.
2. Serve:
   - Pour the smoothie into a bowl and arrange the optional toppings on top.
   - Serve immediately and enjoy with a spoon!

Prep time: 5 minutes. Total time: 5 minutes. Serves: 1

Total Nutrition (per serving): Calories: 482.5; Protein: 6.7g; Carbs: 60.5g; Fat: 28.2g.

Description: This Tropical Sunrise Smoothie Bowl is a refreshing and nutritious breakfast that will transport your taste buds to a sun-drenched paradise. The creamy blend of frozen fruit, banana, coconut milk, and Greek yogurt creates a delicious and satisfying base. Customize your bowl with your favorite toppings for added texture and flavor. In just 5 minutes, you can enjoy a moment of tropical bliss and start your day on a nourishing note.

Ideal for busy mornings, this smoothie bowl offers a quick, healthy, and tasty breakfast option. Packed with vitamins and minerals, it gives you a burst of energy to kickstart your day. The coconut milk and Greek yogurt provide a satisfying start to your morning.

Savory Microwave Breakfast Mug

Ingredients:

- 2 large eggs
- 2 tbsp milk
- 2 tbsp shredded cheddar cheese
- 1 tbsp chopped ham or bacon
- 1 tbsp diced bell pepper
- Salt and pepper to taste
- Optional toppings: sliced green onions, hot sauce

Instructions:

1. In a microwave-safe mug, whisk together eggs and milk.
2. Stir in cheese, ham or bacon, bell pepper, salt, and pepper.
3. Microwave on high for 1 minute, then stir.
4. Microwave for an additional 30-60 seconds until eggs are set.
5. Top with green onions and hot sauce, if desired. Enjoy!

Prep time: 2 minutes. Cook time: 2-3 minutes. Total time: 4-5 minutes. Serves: 1

Total Nutrition (per serving): Calories: 171; Protein: 14g; Carbs: 3.5g; Fat: 10.5g.

Description: This Savory Microwave Breakfast Mug is a quick and tasty solution for busy mornings when you need a nourishing meal in a flash. With protein-packed eggs, savory ham or bacon, and melty cheddar cheese, this satisfying breakfast will keep you fueled for the day ahead.

The addition of diced bell pepper adds a pop of color and freshness to the dish, while the optional toppings of sliced green onions and hot sauce allow you to customize the flavors to your liking. In just a matter of minutes, you can have a delicious and hearty breakfast that will start your day off on the right foot.

Simply whisk the ingredients together in a mug, microwave, and enjoy a comforting breakfast that will satisfy your taste buds and keep you going strong until lunchtime.

Quick Greek Yogurt Parfait with Berries and Granola

Ingredients:
- 1 cup plain Greek yogurt
- 1/4 cup granola
- 1/2 cup mixed fresh berries (strawberries, blueberries, raspberries)
- 1 tablespoon honey
- 1/4 teaspoon vanilla extract
- Optional: 1 tablespoon chia seeds or chopped nuts

Instructions:
1. In a bowl, mix Greek yogurt with honey and vanilla extract.
2. Add granola and berries to the yogurt mixture.
3. Gently fold ingredients together.
4. If using, sprinkle chia seeds or chopped nuts on top.
5. Serve immediately and enjoy your quick, nutritious breakfast!

Prep time: 3-4 minutes. Serves: 1

Total Nutrition (per serving): Calories: 150; Protein: 12g; Carbs: 22.6g; Fat: 7.3g.

Description: This Quick Greek Yogurt Parfait is a delightful and nutritious breakfast that comes together in just minutes. The creamy Greek yogurt provides a protein-rich base, while the crunchy granola and fresh berries add texture and natural sweetness.

The beauty of this parfait lies in its simplicity and adaptability. You can easily swap out the berries for your favorite fruits or use flavored Greek yogurt for variety. The honey adds a touch of sweetness, but you can adjust or omit it to suit your taste.

Perfect for hectic mornings, this parfait can be assembled in mere minutes, offering a balanced meal that will keep you satisfied and energized. It's an ideal solution for those who need a quick, healthy breakfast without sacrificing taste or nutrition.

Breakfast Quesadilla with Spinach and Turkey

Ingredients:
- 1 large whole wheat tortilla
- 2 egg whites (or 1 whole egg)
- 1/4 cup chopped fresh spinach
- 2 oz cooked turkey breast, diced small
- 2 tbsp shredded low-fat cheddar cheese
- 1 tbsp salsa
- Small amount of oil for greasing the pan
- Optional: hot sauce to taste

Instructions:
1. Heat a skillet, add a small amount of oil.
2. Whisk egg whites in a bowl, then pour into the skillet. Add spinach and cook for 1-2 minutes until eggs are set.
3. Place tortilla on top of the egg mixture.
4. Flip everything, then add cooked turkey, cheese, and salsa on one half of the tortilla.
5. Fold tortilla in half, cook for 1-2 minutes per side until golden and cheese melts.
6. Cut into wedges and serve immediately, add hot sauce if desired.

Prep time: 2-3 minutes. Cook time: 7-9 minutes. Total time: 10-12 minutes. Serves: 1

Total Nutrition (per serving): Calories: 327; Protein: 19g; Carbs: 28g; Fat: 15.6g.

Description: This quick Breakfast Quesadilla combines protein-rich eggs, lean turkey, and spinach for a nutritious start. The whole wheat tortilla adds fiber, while cheese and salsa bring flavor. Ready in about 10-12 minutes, it's perfect for busy mornings and can be easily customized to suit your taste.

Gourmet Avocado Toast with Prosciutto and Poached Egg

Ingredients:
- 1 slice artisanal bread (sourdough or whole grain)
- 1/2 ripe avocado
- 1 large egg
- 1 slice prosciutto
- 1 tsp olive oil
- Salt and freshly ground black pepper to taste
- Optional: red pepper flakes, microgreens for garnish

Instructions:
1. Toast the bread to your liking.
2. While bread toasts, bring a small pot of water to a simmer for the egg.
3. Mash avocado and spread on toasted bread. Season with salt and pepper.
4. Poach the egg: crack it into the simmering water, cook for 3 minutes.
5. Layer prosciutto on avocado, top with poached egg.
6. Drizzle with olive oil, add pepper flakes and microgreens if desired.

Prep time: 2-3 minutes. **Cook time:** 4-5 minutes. **Serves:** 1

Total Nutrition (per serving): Calories: 310; Protein: 10g; Carbs: 20g; Fat: 18.5g.

Description: This Gourmet Avocado Toast elevates your breakfast game in less than 10 minutes. The creamy avocado, perfectly poached egg, and savory prosciutto create a restaurant-quality dish at home. It's a balanced meal with healthy fats, protein, and complex carbs to fuel your morning.

Quick to make yet impressive enough for weekend brunch, this versatile recipe can be customized to your taste. The combination of textures and flavors makes every bite a delightful experience, proving that a rushed morning doesn't mean sacrificing taste or nutrition.

Customizable Breakfast Burrito Bowl

Ingredients:

- 1 cup instant brown rice
- 1 cup water
- 1/4 cup black beans, rinsed and drained
- 1 large egg
- 1/4 avocado, diced
- 2 tbsp salsa
- 2 tbsp shredded cheddar cheese
- 1 tbsp chopped cilantro
- Salt and pepper to taste
- Optional: 2 oz cooked chicken, turkey, or bacon bits
- Optional: hot sauce

Instructions:

1. In a microwave-safe bowl, combine instant rice and water. Microwave for 5 minutes, then fluff with a fork.
2. While rice cooks, fry the egg in a small non-stick pan to your preference.
3. If using meat, warm it in the pan after cooking the egg.
4. Layer cooked rice in a bowl, top with black beans and meat (if using).
5. Place the cooked egg on top.
6. Add diced avocado, salsa, and shredded cheese.
7. Sprinkle with cilantro, salt, and pepper.
8. Add hot sauce if desired and serve immediately.

Prep time: 2 minutes. Cook time: 7 minutes. Total time: 9 minutes. Serves: 1

Total Nutrition (per serving): Calories: 450; Protein: 30g; Carbs: 40g; Fat: 18g.

Description: A quick, customizable breakfast bowl with protein-rich egg, fiber-filled brown rice and beans, and heart-healthy avocado. Perfect for busy mornings and easily adaptable to your preferences.

Key Tips for an Efficient Breakfast Setup:

1. Zone Your Space: Create designated areas for different tasks like chopping, cooking, and assembling to streamline your workflow.
2. Prep the Night Before: Set out non-perishable items and tools you'll need in the morning to save precious time.
3. Keep It Clean: Maintain a clutter-free workspace and clean as you go to make the process more enjoyable and efficient.
4. Stock Smart: Always keep your favorite breakfast ingredients well-stocked to avoid last-minute grocery runs.

Must-Have Breakfast Tools and Gadgets:

1. High-speed blender for smoothies and batters.
2. Toaster or toaster oven for bread and bagels.
3. Non-stick skillet for eggs and pancakes.
4. Microwave-safe bowls for quick oatmeal or egg scrambles.
5. Coffee maker or electric kettle for hot beverages.
6. Food processor for chopping nuts or making homemade nut butters.

Egg-cellent Cooking: Your Guide to Perfect Eggs

Quick Guide to Perfect Eggs:

1. Scrambled: Beat eggs with milk. Cook on medium-low (300°F/150°C) for 3-5 minutes, stirring constantly.
2. Fried: Heat pan to medium (350°F/175°C). Cook 2-3 minutes for sunny-side up.
3. Poached: Simmer water (185°F/85°C). Create a whirlpool, slide in egg. Cook 3 minutes.
4. Hard-boiled: Cover eggs with cold water, bring to boil. Remove from heat, cover, let sit 10 minutes. Ice bath after.

Time-Saving Egg Hacks:

1. Meal Prep: Hard-boil a batch on Sunday for the week.
2. Muffin Tin Eggs: Bake at 350°F (175°C) for 12-15 minutes.
3. Easy Peel: Shake boiled eggs in water-filled container for 10 seconds.

This concise guide offers quick, foolproof methods for perfect eggs every time!

Lunchtime Solutions: Quick, Healthy, and Delicious

Welcome to the lunch section of "Healthy and Quick Recipes for Busy People"! In today's fast-paced world, finding time for a nutritious midday meal can often feel like an insurmountable challenge. Whether you're racing against deadlines at the office, managing a hectic household, or juggling multiple responsibilities, lunch can easily become an afterthought. But fear not! We've curated a collection of lunches that are not only quick to prepare but also packed with the nutrients you need to power through your afternoon.

In this section, you'll discover 15 lunch recipes designed to be made in 20 minutes or less. From crisp salads and satisfying sandwiches to warm soups and protein-rich bowls, these meals will keep you energized without sacrificing taste or nutrition. Each recipe balances protein, complex carbohydrates, and healthy fats to maintain steady energy levels throughout your day.

Why is a good lunch so important? It's more than just a break in your day – it's fuel for your body and mind. A well-balanced lunch can improve concentration, boost productivity, and help maintain a healthy weight. It's an opportunity to nourish yourself with vital nutrients and recharge for the tasks ahead.

Our recipes are designed with busy professionals, parents, and students in mind. We understand that you may not have access to a full kitchen during lunchtime, so many of our recipes can be prepared in advance or quickly assembled with minimal equipment. Some can even be enjoyed cold or at room temperature, perfect for those days when you can't step away from your desk or don't have access to a microwave.

Tips for Successful Lunches:
1. Prep smartly: Spend 15 minutes the night before washing and chopping vegetables for the next day's lunch.
   This small time investment can save precious minutes during your busy mornings.

2. Invest in quality containers: Good storage keeps ingredients fresh and makes transportation hassle-free. Look for leak-proof, microwave-safe containers with compartments to keep different components separate.
3. Plan for extras: When cooking dinner, prepare a bit extra to pack for tomorrow's lunch. It's efficient and ensures a fresh, homemade meal without additional effort.
4. Stock your pantry: Keep items like canned beans, tuna, and quick-cook grains on hand for last-minute lunches. These staples can form the base of a nutritious meal in no time.
5. Prioritize vegetables: Aim to include at least one serving of vegetables in every lunch for essential nutrients and fiber. Not only will this boost your health, but it will also add color and variety to your meals.
6. Mix and match: Our recipes are flexible – feel free to swap ingredients based on your preferences or what's in your fridge. This approach prevents boredom and allows you to use up what you have on hand.
7. Don't forget hydration: Pack a reusable water bottle with your lunch to ensure you stay hydrated throughout the day. Proper hydration is key to maintaining energy and focus.
8. Balance your plate: Try to include a source of lean protein, complex carbohydrates, and healthy fats in each lunch.

Remember, a nutritious lunch isn't just about satisfying hunger—it's about fueling your body and mind for peak afternoon performance. These recipes are designed to be both nourishing and exciting, proving that healthy eating can be delicious and convenient, even on the busiest of days.

Let's explore these time-saving, mouthwatering lunch recipes that will transform your midday meals, boost your productivity, and make you look forward to lunchtime every day. Get ready to revolutionize your lunch routine and discover just how satisfying and simple healthy eating can be!

Quick Caprese Pasta Salad

Ingredients:

- 2 cups whole wheat pasta (rotini or penne)
- 1 cup cherry tomatoes, halved
- 4 oz fresh mozzarella, cubed
- 1/4 cup fresh basil leaves, chopped
- 2 tbsp extra virgin olive oil
- 1 tbsp balsamic vinegar
- Salt and pepper to taste
- Optional: 2 tbsp pine nuts

Instructions:

1. Cook pasta according to package instructions. Drain and rinse with cold water.
2. In a large bowl, combine cooled pasta, tomatoes, mozzarella, and basil.
3. In a small bowl, whisk together olive oil, balsamic vinegar, salt, and pepper.
4. Pour dressing over pasta mixture and toss gently to combine.
5. If using, sprinkle pine nuts on top.
6. Serve immediately or refrigerate for up to 4 hours.

Prep time: 10 minutes. Cook time: 10 minutes. Total time: 20 minutes. Serves: 2

Total Nutrition (per serving): Calories: 300; Protein: 12g; Carbs: 40g; Fat: 10g.

Description: This Quick Caprese Pasta Salad offers a refreshing twist on a classic Italian dish. Ready in just 20 minutes, it's perfect for busy days. The combination of whole wheat pasta, juicy tomatoes, creamy mozzarella, and fragrant basil creates a delicious balance of flavors and textures. Enjoy it warm right away or refrigerate for later - it tastes great either way!

Speedy Southwest Chicken Wrap

Ingredients:

- 1 large whole wheat tortilla
- 1/2 cup shredded rotisserie chicken
- 1/4 cup black beans, rinsed and drained
- 1/4 cup corn kernels
- 1/4 avocado, sliced
- 2 tbsp salsa
- 2 tbsp plain Greek yogurt
- 1/4 cup shredded lettuce
- 2 tbsp shredded cheddar cheese
- Optional: hot sauce to taste

Instructions:

1. Lay the tortilla flat on a clean surface.
2. Spread Greek yogurt in the center of the tortilla.
3. Layer chicken, black beans, corn, avocado slices, and lettuce.
4. Top with salsa, cheddar cheese, and hot sauce if using.
5. Fold in the sides of the tortilla and roll tightly.
6. Cut in half diagonally and serve immediately.

Prep time: 5-7 minutes. Total time: 5-7 minutes. Serves: 1

Total Nutrition (per serving): Calories: 420; Protein: 28g; Carbs: 38g; Fat: 18g.

Description: This Speedy Southwest Chicken Wrap is perfect for busy lunch hours. Packed with protein from the chicken and beans, it provides long-lasting energy. The avocado adds healthy fats, while the vegetables contribute essential nutrients and fiber. Using rotisserie chicken saves time without sacrificing flavor or nutrition. Ideal for office lunches or quick meals at home, this wrap can be assembled in minutes and is easily customizable.

Speedy Tuna & Avocado Power Bowl

Ingredients:
- 1 can (5 oz) tuna in water, drained
- 1/2 avocado, diced
- 1/2 cup cherry tomatoes, halved
- 1/4 cup canned corn, drained
- 1/4 cup canned black beans, drained and rinsed
- 1 cup pre-washed mixed salad greens
- 1 tbsp olive oil
- 1 tbsp lemon juice
- Salt and pepper to taste
- Optional: hot sauce to taste

Instructions:
1. In a bowl, combine tuna, avocado, tomatoes, corn, and black beans.
2. Add mixed salad greens on top.
3. Drizzle with olive oil and lemon juice.
4. Season with salt and pepper. Add hot sauce if desired.
5. Gently toss all ingredients together and enjoy!

Prep time: 5-7 minutes. Total time: 5-7 minutes. Serves: 1

Total Nutrition (per serving): Calories: 350; Protein: 25g; Carbs: 22g; Fat: 15g.

Description: This Speedy Tuna & Avocado Power Bowl is the ultimate quick-fix for a nutritious and satisfying lunch. Packed with protein from tuna, healthy fats from avocado, and a rainbow of vegetables, this bowl will keep you energized all afternoon. Perfect for busy professionals, it proves that nutritious eating doesn't have to be time-consuming or complicated. The combination of flavors and textures makes every bite exciting and it's easily customizable.

5-Minute Creamy Tomato Soup with Grilled Cheese Croutons

Ingredients:
- 1 can (14.5 oz) crushed tomatoes
- 1/2 cup milk
- 1/4 tsp garlic powder
- 1/4 tsp dried basil
- Salt and pepper to taste
- 1 slice whole grain bread
- 2 tbsp shredded cheddar cheese

Instructions:
1. In a microwave-safe bowl, combine tomatoes, milk, garlic powder, and basil.
2. Microwave on high for 3 minutes, stirring halfway through.
3. While soup heats, toast the bread and top with cheese.
4. Broil the cheese toast for 1 minute until bubbly.
5. Cut the cheese toast into small cubes.
6. Season soup with salt and pepper, top with cheese croutons.

Prep time: 2 minutes. Cook time: 4 minutes. Total time: 6 minutes. Serves: 1

Total Nutrition (per serving): Calories: 284; Protein: 10g; Carbs: 32g; Fat: 12g.

Description: This 5-Minute Creamy Tomato Soup is the ultimate comfort food for busy days. The rich, velvety texture and classic flavor will transport you back to childhood, but with a gourmet twist. The grilled cheese croutons add a fun, crunchy element that makes this soup irresistible.

Perfect for cold days or when you need a quick pick-me-up, this soup proves that homemade doesn't have to mean time-consuming. It's a hug in a bowl that you can make in less time than it takes to order takeout!

Quick and Healthy
Customizable Noodle Soup

Ingredients:
- 2 cups water
- 1 cup whole wheat pasta (small shapes like orzo or small shells)
- 1 cup mixed frozen vegetables
- 1 tsp vegetable bouillon powder
- 1/4 tsp dried herbs (like basil or oregano)
- Salt and pepper to taste
- Optional protein: 1/2 cup diced cooked chicken or ham

Instructions:
1. In a medium pot, bring water to a boil.
2. Add pasta, frozen vegetables, bouillon powder, and dried herbs.
3. Reduce heat to medium and simmer for 8-10 minutes, until pasta is tender.
4. If using, add diced chicken or ham in the last 2 minutes of cooking.
5. Season with salt and pepper to taste.
6. Serve hot.

Prep time: 2 minutes. Cook time: 10 minutes. Total time: 12 minutes. Serves: 1

Total Nutrition (per serving): Calories: 210; Protein: 8g; Carbs: 34g; Fat: 4g.

Description: This Quick and Healthy Customizable Noodle Soup is perfect for busy days when you need a nourishing meal in minutes. The whole wheat pasta and vegetables provide a good balance of complex carbohydrates and nutrients, while the optional protein makes it more filling. It's a versatile recipe that you can easily adapt to your preferences or what you have on hand. Whether you're a vegetarian or a meat-eater, this soup offers a satisfying and warming meal that's both quick to make and easy to clean up after.

5-Minute Mediterranean Chickpea Salad

Ingredients:

- 1 can (15 oz) chickpeas, drained and rinsed
- 1/2 cup cherry tomatoes, halved
- 1/4 cup cucumber, diced
- 2 tbsp red onion, finely chopped
- 2 tbsp crumbled feta cheese
- 1 tbsp olive oil
- 1 tbsp lemon juice
- 1 tsp dried oregano
- Salt and pepper to taste
- Optional: 1 tbsp chopped fresh parsley

Instructions:

1. In a medium bowl, combine chickpeas, tomatoes, cucumber, red onion, and feta cheese.
2. In a small bowl, whisk together olive oil, lemon juice, and oregano.
3. Pour the dressing over the salad and toss gently to combine.
4. Season with salt and pepper to taste.
5. If using, sprinkle chopped parsley on top.
6. Serve immediately or refrigerate for up to 2 hours before eating.

Prep time: 5 minutes. Total time: 5 minutes. Serves: 1-2

Total Nutrition (per serving): Calories: 280; Protein: 8g; Carbs: 40g; Fat: 10g.

Description: This 5-Minute Mediterranean Chickpea Salad is a quick and refreshing meal perfect for busy days. Packed with protein-rich chickpeas and crisp vegetables, it offers a satisfying crunch and a burst of flavors. The tangy feta and zesty lemon dressing bring a taste of the Mediterranean to your lunch break. It's an ideal option for those looking for a no-cook meal that's both nutritious and delicious. Easy to prepare ahead and portable, this salad is a great alternative to sandwiches or fast food. Enjoy it as is, or serve it over a bed of greens for an even more substantial meal.

15-Minute Honey Garlic Glazed Salmon Bowl

Ingredients:
- 1 salmon fillet (4-6 oz)
- 2 tbsp honey
- 2 tbsp soy sauce
- 2 cloves garlic, minced
- 1 cup instant rice
- 1 cup water
- 1 cup broccoli florets
- 1 tbsp olive oil
- Lemon wedge for serving
- Optional: sesame seeds for garnish

Instructions:
1. In a small bowl, mix honey, soy sauce, and minced garlic.
2. Heat olive oil in a non-stick pan over medium-high heat.
3. Cook salmon for 3-4 minutes each side, until golden.
4. Pour honey garlic mixture over salmon, cook for 1 minute until glazed.
5. Meanwhile, prepare rice according to package instructions for microwave cooking.
6. Steam broccoli in the microwave for 2-3 minutes until tender-crisp.
7. Assemble bowl: rice, broccoli, and glazed salmon. Drizzle with remaining sauce.
8. Garnish with lemon wedge and optional sesame seeds.

Prep time: 5 minutes. Cook time: 10 minutes. Total time: 15 minutes. Serves: 1

Total Nutrition (per serving): Calories: 450; Protein: 25g; Carbs: 35g; Fat: 20g.

Description: This 15-Minute Honey Garlic Glazed Salmon Bowl is a game-changer for quick, restaurant-quality meals at home. The salmon, perfectly seared and coated in a sweet and savory glaze, is the star of this dish. Paired with fluffy rice and crisp broccoli, it's a balanced meal that looks and tastes like it took much longer to prepare. The honey garlic glaze adds a gourmet touch with its perfect blend of flavors.

15-Minute Loaded Baked Potato

Ingredients:
- 1 large russet potato
- 2 tbsp shredded cheddar cheese
- 2 tbsp plain Greek yogurt
- 2 slices bacon, cooked and crumbled
- 1 green onion, chopped
- Salt and pepper to taste

Instructions:
1. Wash potato and prick several times with a fork.
2. Microwave on high for 5 minutes, turn over, cook for another 3-5 minutes until soft.
3. Cut potato in half, fluff the inside with a fork.
4. Top with cheese, Greek yogurt, bacon, and green onion.
5. Season with salt and pepper.

Prep time: 2 minutes. Cook time: 8-10 minutes. Total time: 10-12 minutes. Serves: 1

Total Nutrition (per serving): Calories: 420; Protein: 13g; Carbs: 70g; Fat: 14g.

Description: This 15-Minute Loaded Baked Potato offers all the comfort of a classic American dish in a fraction of the time. The fluffy potato is perfectly complemented by melty cheese, tangy Greek yogurt (a healthier alternative to sour cream), crispy bacon, and fresh green onions. It's a satisfying, customizable meal that's perfect for a quick lunch or easy dinner. The microwave method makes it accessible even in office settings.

Note: This recipe assumes you have pre-cooked bacon on hand. If not, you can quickly cook the bacon in the microwave while the potato is cooking. Place bacon slices between paper towels on a microwave-safe plate and cook for about 1 minute per slice, or until crispy.

15-Minute Skillet Caprese Chicken

Ingredients:
- 2 small chicken breasts (about 6 oz each)
- 1 cup cherry tomatoes, halved
- 1 cup fresh mozzarella pearls
- 1/4 cup fresh basil leaves, chopped
- 2 tbsp balsamic glaze
- 1 tbsp olive oil
- Salt and pepper to taste
- 1 tsp Italian seasoning

Instructions:
1. Season chicken with salt, pepper, and Italian seasoning.
2. Heat olive oil in a skillet over medium-high heat.
3. Cook chicken for 4-5 minutes each side until golden and cooked through.
4. Remove chicken, let rest for 2 minutes, then slice.
5. In the same skillet, add tomatoes and cook for 1-2 minutes.
6. Return chicken to skillet, add mozzarella and basil.
7. Drizzle with balsamic glaze and serve.

Prep time: 5 minutes. Cook time: 10 minutes. Total time: 15 minutes. Serves: 2

Total Nutrition (per serving): Calories: 380; Protein: 35g; Carbs: 10g; Fat: 20g.

Description: This 15-Minute Skillet Caprese Chicken transforms simple ingredients into a restaurant-quality meal. The golden-brown chicken pairs perfectly with burst tomatoes, creamy mozzarella, and aromatic basil. The balsamic glaze adds a touch of sweetness and tang, elevating the dish to gourmet status. It's a one-pan wonder that's both impressive and easy, ideal for busy weeknights or when you want to impress without the stress. This recipe proves that fresh, delicious meals can be made quickly at home.

15-Minute Crispy Potato and Sausage Skillet

Ingredients:
- 2 medium potatoes, diced into 1/2-inch cubes
- 1 pre-cooked sausage, sliced
- 1/2 small onion, diced
- 1 clove garlic, minced
- 1 tbsp olive oil
- 1 tsp paprika
- 1 tsp dried thyme
- Salt and pepper to taste
- 2 tbsp chopped fresh parsley

Instructions:
1. Heat olive oil in a large skillet over medium-high heat.
2. Add potatoes, season with salt, pepper, paprika, and thyme. Cook for 5 minutes, stirring occasionally.
3. Add onions and garlic, cook for another 3 minutes.
4. Add sliced sausage, cook for 5 minutes until potatoes are crispy and sausage is browned.
5. Sprinkle with fresh parsley before serving.

Prep time: 5 minutes. Cook time: 10 minutes. Total time: 15 minutes. Serves: 2

Total Nutrition (per serving): Calories: 490; Protein: 18g; Carbs: 45g; Fat: 25g.

Description: This 15-Minute Crispy Potato and Sausage Skillet is a hearty, satisfying meal that's perfect for busy days. The crispy potatoes and savory sausage create a delicious combination that's both comforting and quick to prepare. It's ideal for weeknight dinners or a speedy lunch. Feel free to use your favorite type of sausage or swap in different herbs for variety. This one-pan wonder proves that fast food can be homemade, delicious, and adaptable to your tastes.

12-Minute Lemon Garlic Shrimp Pasta

Ingredients:

- 4 oz spaghetti or linguine
- 1/2 lb medium shrimp, peeled and deveined
- 2 tbsp olive oil
- 3 cloves garlic, minced
- 1 lemon, juiced and zested
- 1/4 tsp red pepper flakes
- 2 tbsp fresh parsley, chopped
- Salt and pepper to taste

Instructions:

1. Cook pasta according to package instructions. Reserve 1/4 cup pasta water before draining.
2. While pasta cooks, heat olive oil in a large skillet over medium heat.
3. Add garlic and red pepper flakes, cook for 30 seconds until fragrant.
4. Add shrimp, cook for 2-3 minutes per side until pink.
5. Add lemon juice, zest, and pasta water. Simmer for 1 minute.
6. Toss in cooked pasta and parsley. Season with salt and pepper.

Prep time: 4 minutes. Cook time: 8 minutes. Total time: 12 minutes. Serves: 2

Total Nutrition (per serving): Calories: 350; Protein: 25g; Carbs: 40g; Fat: 8g.

Description: This 12-Minute Lemon Garlic Shrimp Pasta is a perfect quick meal for busy weeknights. The combination of zesty lemon, aromatic garlic, and succulent shrimp creates a light yet satisfying dish. The touch of heat from red pepper flakes adds depth, while fresh parsley brings brightness. It's a restaurant-quality meal that comes together in minutes, proving that fast food can be both elegant and homemade. Ideal for those looking for a quick, impressive dinner without sacrificing flavor or nutrition.

12–Minute Teriyaki Chicken Stir-Fry Bowl

Ingredients:
- 1 chicken breast, cut into bite-sized pieces
- 2 cups mixed frozen vegetables
- 1/4 cup teriyaki sauce
- 1 tbsp vegetable oil
- 1 cup instant rice
- 1 green onion, sliced
- 1 tsp sesame seeds

Instructions:
1. Cook instant rice according to package instructions.
2. Heat oil in a large skillet over medium-high heat.
3. Add chicken, cook for 4-5 minutes until golden.
4. Add frozen vegetables and teriyaki sauce, stir-fry for 3-4 minutes.
5. Serve over rice, garnish with green onions and sesame seeds.

Prep time: 3 minutes. Cook time: 9 minutes. Total time: 12 minutes. Serves: 2

Total Nutrition (per serving): Calories: 320; Protein: 30g; Carbs: 40g; Fat: 8g.

Description: This 12-Minute Teriyaki Chicken Stir-Fry Bowl is a quick and flavorful meal perfect for busy weeknights. The tender chicken and crisp vegetables, coated in savory-sweet teriyaki sauce, create a satisfying and balanced dish. Served over fluffy rice and topped with fresh green onions and sesame seeds, it offers a restaurant-quality experience in minutes. This recipe proves that a delicious, homemade Asian-inspired meal can be faster than takeout.

Smart Solutions for Effortless Lunches

1. Batch cooking basics: • Cook extra proteins on weekends for easy weekday use • Prepare a large salad base to last several days • Make versatile grain bowls that can be customized daily
2. Mason jar meals: • Layer salads with dressing at the bottom, greens on top • Create parfaits with yogurt, fruit, and granola • Assemble noodle soups with broth added just before eating
3. Bento box inspiration: • Use silicone cupcake liners to separate foods • Include a mix of proteins, grains, fruits, and vegetables • Add a small treat for a balanced, satisfying meal
4. No-heat lunch ideas: • Wraps with hummus, veggies, and cold cuts • Cheese and cracker plates with nuts and dried fruits • Cold pasta or grain salads with vinaigrette dressing

Quick Tips for Lunch Success

1. Freezer-friendly options: • Individually wrap burritos for easy grab-and-go • Freeze soups in portion-sized containers • Make and freeze mini quiches in muffin tins
2. Repurposing leftovers: • Transform dinner meats into lunch sandwiches or salads • Use leftover rice for quick fried rice or rice pudding • Blend cooked vegetables into creamy soups
3. Smart storage solutions: • Use divided containers to keep foods separate • Invest in a good quality insulated lunch bag • Pack dressings and sauces separately to prevent sogginess
4. Quick assembly techniques: • Create a lunch packing station in your fridge • Pre-portion snacks into small containers for the week • Keep a variety of pre-washed greens on hand
5. Hydration hacks: • Freeze water bottles to use as ice packs • Infuse water with fruits for natural flavoring • Pack herbal tea bags for a comforting afternoon drink

Dinnertime Delights: Quick and Nutritious Evening Meals

Welcome to the dinner section of our cookbook! After a long day, the last thing you want is to spend hours in the kitchen. That's why we've curated a collection of delicious, nutritious, and most importantly, quick dinner recipes that will satisfy your hunger without eating up your evening.

In this section, you'll find 12 dinner recipes designed to be prepared in 30 minutes or less. From one-pan wonders to sheet pan suppers, these meals are crafted to minimize prep time and cleanup while maximizing flavor and nutrition. Whether you're cooking for one, feeding a family, or entertaining friends, these recipes are adaptable to your needs.

Why Quick Dinners Matter: In our fast-paced world, quick dinners are more than just a convenience—they're a necessity. But quick doesn't mean sacrificing health or taste. Our recipes prove that you can have a balanced, delicious meal on the table in less time than it takes to order takeout. By cooking at home, you control the ingredients, portions, and nutrition, all while saving money.

Tips for Successful Quick Dinners:

- Prep Ahead: Spend some time on the weekend chopping vegetables or marinating meats to save time during the week. Store prepped ingredients in clear containers in your fridge for easy access.
- Embrace One-Pot Meals: These dishes reduce cleanup time and often taste even better the next day as leftovers. Plus, they're great for combining proteins, vegetables, and grains in one dish.
- Keep a Well-Stocked Pantry: Having staples like canned tomatoes, pasta, rice, and spices on hand means you're always ready to whip up a quick meal. Regularly update your pantry inventory to ensure you have what you need.
- Use Your Freezer Wisely: Freeze portions of cooked grains, sauces, or even entire meals for busy nights. Properly labeled and dated freezer meals can be a lifesaver on hectic evenings.

- Don't Shy Away from Shortcuts: Pre-cut vegetables, rotisserie chicken, or jarred sauces can be lifesavers on hectic evenings. Just be mindful of added sodium or preservatives in some convenience products.
- Master the Art of Meal Planning: Plan your dinners for the week ahead. This not only saves time but also reduces stress and helps with grocery shopping.
- Invest in Time-Saving Tools: A good set of sharp knives, a reliable food processor, and an instant-read thermometer can significantly speed up your cooking process.
- Learn to Multitask in the Kitchen: While your main dish is cooking, prepare a quick side salad or set the table. Efficient use of your time can help get dinner on the table faster.
- Don't Forget About Breakfast for Dinner: Eggs, pancakes, or a quick frittata can make for a satisfying and easy evening meal.
- Keep It Simple: On the busiest nights, remember that a simple combination of a protein, a vegetable, and a whole grain can make a perfectly balanced meal.

Remember, a nutritious dinner doesn't have to be complicated or time-consuming. With these recipes and tips, you'll be able to put a delicious meal on the table in no time, leaving you more time to relax and enjoy your evening. Cooking should be a joy, not a chore, and these quick dinner ideas are designed to bring that joy back into your kitchen, even on the busiest of days.

Let's dive into these mouthwatering dinner recipes that prove fast can be fantastic! From sizzling stir-fries to comforting pasta dishes, and from zesty salads to hearty one-pot wonders, these meals will revolutionize your weeknight dinner routine. Get ready to impress yourself and your loved ones with minimal effort and maximum flavor!

Grilled Herb Chicken with Mixed Vegetable Salad

Ingredients:
- 2 chicken breasts
- 2 tbsp olive oil
- 1 tsp dried herbs (thyme, rosemary, oregano mix)
- 2 cups mixed vegetables (tomatoes, cucumbers, bell peppers)
- 1/4 red onion, thinly sliced
- 1 tbsp lemon juice
- Salt and pepper to taste

Instructions:
1. Season chicken with herbs, salt, and pepper.
2. Grill chicken for 6-7 minutes per side until cooked through.
3. Chop vegetables and mix with sliced onion.
4. Dress salad with lemon juice and 1 tbsp olive oil.
5. Serve grilled chicken alongside the fresh vegetable salad.

Prep time: 5 minutes. **Cook time:** 15 minutes. **Serves:** 2

Total Nutrition (per serving): Calories: 320; Protein: 30g; Carbs: 10g; Fat: 15g.

Description: This Grilled Herb Chicken with Mixed Vegetable Salad is a perfect quick and healthy dinner option. The herb-seasoned chicken provides lean protein, while the colorful vegetable salad adds essential nutrients and fiber. This light yet satisfying meal is ideal for busy weeknights when you want a nutritious dinner without spending hours in the kitchen. The fresh flavors and simple preparation make it a go-to recipe for maintaining a balanced diet even with a hectic schedule.

Lemon Garlic Shrimp with Tomato and Spinach Salad

Ingredients:

- 12 large shrimp, peeled and deveined
- 1 tbsp olive oil
- 2 cloves garlic, minced
- 1 lemon, juiced and zested
- 2 cups baby spinach
- 1 cup cherry tomatoes, halved
- 1/4 red onion, thinly sliced
- 1 tbsp balsamic vinegar
- Salt and pepper to taste

Instructions:

1. Toss shrimp with 1/2 tbsp oil, garlic, lemon zest.
2. Grill shrimp for 2-3 minutes per side until pink.
3. Mix spinach, tomatoes, and onion in a bowl.
4. Whisk remaining oil with balsamic vinegar and lemon juice.
5. Toss salad with dressing, top with grilled shrimp.

Prep time: 5 minutes. Cook time: 6 minutes. Serves: 2

Total Nutrition (per serving): Calories: 310; Protein: 28g; Carbs: 12g; Fat: 15g.

Description: This Lemon Garlic Shrimp with Tomato and Spinach Salad offers a delightful blend of flavors suitable for all palates. The zesty lemon-garlic shrimp provides lean protein, while the fresh salad adds a variety of textures and nutrients. Ready in just 11 minutes, this meal is perfect for busy individuals seeking a quick, healthy dinner option. The light, refreshing taste makes it ideal for any season, and it's easily customizable to suit different preferences. Enjoy a restaurant-quality meal at home without the fuss!

Colorful Mediterranean Chopped Salad with Grilled Chicken

Ingredients:
- 1 chicken breast, grilled and sliced
- 2 cups mixed salad greens
- 1/2 cup cherry tomatoes, halved
- 1/2 cucumber, diced
- 1/4 red onion, thinly sliced
- 1/4 cup kalamata olives, pitted
- 1/4 cup feta cheese, crumbled
- 2 tbsp extra virgin olive oil
- 1 tbsp lemon juice
- 1 tsp dried oregano
- Salt and pepper to taste

Instructions:
1. Grill chicken breast, let cool slightly, then slice.
2. In a large bowl, combine greens, tomatoes, cucumber, and onion.
3. Add olives and feta cheese to the salad.
4. Whisk olive oil, lemon juice, oregano, salt, and pepper.
5. Toss salad with dressing, top with sliced chicken.

Prep time: 10 minutes. Cook time: 10 minutes. Serves: 2

Total Nutrition (per serving): Calories: 350; Protein: 32g; Carbs: 20g; Fat: 15g.

Description: This Colorful Mediterranean Chopped Salad with Grilled Chicken is a refreshing and satisfying dinner option. Packed with vibrant vegetables, tangy feta, and lean protein, it offers a perfect balance of flavors and nutrients. The zesty lemon-oregano dressing ties all the ingredients together beautifully. This salad is ideal for warm evenings or when you're craving a light yet filling meal. It's quick to prepare, making it perfect for busy individuals who don't want to compromise on taste or nutrition. Enjoy a taste of the Mediterranean in just 20 minutes!

Crispy Sheet Pan Gnocchi with Roasted Vegetables

Ingredients:
- 1 package (16 oz) shelf-stable gnocchi
- 2 cups mixed vegetables (cherry tomatoes, zucchini, bell peppers)
- 1 red onion, cut into wedges
- 3 tbsp olive oil
- 2 cloves garlic, minced
- 1 tsp dried Italian herbs
- Salt and pepper to taste
- 1/4 cup grated Parmesan cheese
- Fresh basil leaves for garnish

Instructions:
1. Preheat oven to 425°F (220°C).
2. Toss gnocchi, vegetables, oil, garlic, herbs, salt, and pepper on a baking sheet.
3. Spread in a single layer and roast for 20-25 minutes, stirring halfway.
4. Sprinkle with Parmesan and broil for 2-3 minutes until golden.
5. Garnish with fresh basil before serving.

Prep time: 5 minutes. Cook time: 25 minutes. Serves: 2

Total Nutrition (per serving): Calories: 400; Protein: 10g; Carbs: 60g; Fat: 15g.

Description: This Crispy Sheet Pan Gnocchi with Roasted Vegetables is a game-changer for busy weeknights. The magic happens as the gnocchi transforms from soft pillows to crispy, golden bites in the oven – no boiling required! Paired with colorful roasted vegetables and topped with nutty Parmesan, this dish offers a perfect balance of textures and flavors. It's a one-pan wonder that's not only delicious but also incredibly easy to prepare and clean up. Ideal for those seeking a comforting yet healthy meal with minimal effort.

Honey Mustard Glazed Pork Chops with Apple Slaw

Ingredients:
- 2 boneless pork chops (6 oz each)
- 2 tbsp honey
- 1 tbsp Dijon mustard
- 1 tsp apple cider vinegar
- 1 apple, julienned
- 2 cups shredded cabbage
- 2 tbsp mayonnaise
- 1 tbsp lemon juice
- Salt and pepper to taste

Instructions:
1. Mix honey, mustard, and vinegar for glaze.
2. Season pork chops with salt and pepper.
3. Grill or pan-fry chops 4-5 minutes per side, brushing with glaze.
4. For slaw, mix apple, cabbage, mayo, and lemon juice.
5. Let chops rest 3 minutes, then serve with slaw.

Prep time: 10 minutes. Cook time: 15 minutes. Serves: 2

Total Nutrition (per serving): Calories: 450; Protein: 30g; Carbs: 35g; Fat: 20g.

Description: These Honey Mustard Glazed Pork Chops with Apple Slaw offer a perfect balance of sweet, tangy, and savory flavors. The glaze caramelizes beautifully on the pork, while the crisp, refreshing slaw provides a delightful contrast. Ready in just 25 minutes, this dish is ideal for busy weeknights when you want a restaurant-quality meal without the fuss. The combination of lean protein and vegetable-based side makes for a satisfying, nutritious dinner that's sure to impress.

Creamy Garlic Turkey Skillet with Herbed Mashed Potatoes

Ingredients:

- 1 lb turkey breast, cut into thin strips
- 2 cups potato, peeled and cubed
- 1/4 cup milk or cream (for mashing)
- 1/2 cup heavy cream (for sauce)
- 2 tbsp butter
- 2 cloves garlic, minced
- 1 tsp dried thyme
- 1/2 cup water
- 1 tsp bouillon powder
- 1 tbsp olive oil
- Salt and pepper to taste
- Fresh parsley, chopped

Instructions:

1. Boil potatoes until tender, about 15 minutes.
2. Season turkey, cook in oil until golden, 5-6 minutes.
3. Remove turkey, sauté garlic 1 minute.
4. Add water, bouillon, cream, thyme. Simmer 3-4 minutes.
5. Return turkey to skillet, coat with sauce.
6. Mash potatoes with butter, milk/cream, salt, pepper.
7. Serve turkey over potatoes, garnish with parsley.

Prep time: 5 minutes. Cook time: 20 minutes. Serves: 4

Total Nutrition (per serving): Calories: 500; Protein: 35g; Carbs: 45g; Fat: 20g.

Description: This Creamy Garlic Turkey Skillet with Herbed Mashed Potatoes offers comfort in a quick, 25-minute meal. Tender turkey in a rich sauce pairs perfectly with fluffy potatoes. It's ideal for busy nights when you crave homemade goodness without lengthy cooking.

Crispy Honey-Garlic Beef Stir-Fry with Rice

Ingredients:

- 1 lb beef sirloin or veal cutlets, thinly sliced
- 2 tbsp cornstarch
- 3 tbsp soy sauce
- 2 tbsp honey
- 4 cloves garlic, minced
- 1 tbsp vegetable oil
- 2 cups mixed vegetables (bell peppers, broccoli, carrots)
- 1 cup uncooked long-grain rice (such as jasmine or basmati)
- 2 cups water
- 2 green onions, sliced
- Sesame seeds for garnish

Instructions:

1. Combine rice and water in a pot. Bring to boil, reduce heat, simmer covered for 18-20 minutes.
2. Toss beef or veal with cornstarch, set aside.
3. Mix soy sauce, honey, and garlic in a bowl.
4. Heat oil in a large skillet over high heat.
5. Cook meat in batches until crispy, 2-3 minutes (1-2 minutes for veal).
6. Remove meat, stir-fry vegetables for 3-4 minutes.
7. Return meat to skillet, add sauce, cook 1-2 minutes.
8. Fluff rice with a fork. Serve the stir-fry over the rice, then garnish with sliced green onions and sprinkle with sesame seeds.

Prep time: 10 minutes. Cook time: 20 minutes. Serves: 4

Total Nutrition (per serving): Calories: 450; Protein: 28g; Carbs: 50g; Fat: 15g.

Description: This Crispy Honey-Garlic Stir-Fry with Rice offers crispy meat and colorful veggies coated in a sweet-savory sauce, served over fluffy rice. Ready in 30 minutes, it's faster than takeout and much healthier.

Sheet Pan Lemon Herb Salmon
with Roasted Asparagus

Ingredients:
- 4 salmon fillets (6 oz each)
- 1 lb asparagus, trimmed
- 2 tbsp olive oil
- 2 lemons (1 juiced, 1 sliced)
- 2 cloves garlic, minced
- 1 tsp dried oregano
- 1 tsp dried thyme
- Salt and pepper to taste
- 2 tbsp fresh parsley, chopped

Instructions:
1. Preheat oven to 400°F (200°C). Line a baking sheet with parchment paper.
2. Place salmon and asparagus on the sheet.
3. Mix oil, lemon juice, garlic, oregano, thyme, salt, and pepper in a bowl.
4. Brush mixture over salmon and asparagus.
5. Top salmon with lemon slices.
6. Bake for 12-15 minutes until salmon is cooked and asparagus is tender.
7. Garnish with fresh parsley before serving.

Prep time: 10 minutes. Cook time: 15 minutes. Serves: 4

Total Nutrition (per serving): Calories: 400; Protein: 35g; Carbs: 10g; Fat: 25g.

Description: This Sheet Pan Lemon Herb Salmon with Roasted Asparagus is a perfect weeknight dinner for busy Americans. It's packed with flavor, nutrients, and best of all, it's ready in just 25 minutes with minimal cleanup. The lemony, herb-infused salmon pairs beautifully with crisp-tender asparagus, creating a balanced and satisfying meal. It's an ideal option for those looking to incorporate more fish into their diet without spending hours in the kitchen.

Southwestern Chicken and Black Bean Skillet

Ingredients:

- 1 lb boneless, skinless chicken breasts, diced
- 1 can (15 oz) black beans, drained and rinsed
- 1 cup corn kernels (fresh, frozen, or canned)
- 1 red bell pepper, diced
- 1 small onion, diced
- 2 cloves garlic, minced
- 1 can (14.5 oz) diced tomatoes
- 1 tbsp olive oil
- 2 tsp chili powder
- 1 tsp ground cumin
- Salt and pepper to taste
- 1 cup shredded cheddar cheese
- 2 tbsp fresh cilantro, chopped

Instructions:

1. Heat oil in a large skillet over medium-high heat.
2. Add chicken, cook until browned, about 5 minutes.
3. Add onion, bell pepper, and garlic. Cook for 3 minutes.
4. Stir in beans, corn, tomatoes, chili powder, and cumin.
5. Simmer for 5 minutes, stirring occasionally.
6. Top with cheese, cover until melted, about 2 minutes.
7. Garnish with cilantro before serving.

Prep time: 10 minutes. Cook time: 15 minutes. Serves: 4

Total Nutrition (per serving): Calories: 420; Protein: 38g; Carbs: 30g; Fat: 18g.

Description: This Southwestern Chicken and Black Bean Skillet is a flavorful one-pan wonder perfect for busy weeknights. Packed with protein and vegetables, it offers a balanced meal with minimal cleanup. The combination of spices gives it a delicious Tex-Mex flavor that's sure to be a hit with the family.

Super Crispy Potato-Parmesan Crusted Chicken

Ingredients:

- 4 thin chicken cutlets (or 2 chicken breasts, butterflied and halved)
- 1 cup instant mashed potato flakes
- 1/2 cup grated Parmesan cheese
- 1 tsp garlic powder
- 1 tsp dried oregano
- 1/2 tsp paprika
- Salt and pepper to taste
- 2 large eggs, beaten
- 2 tbsp olive oil

Instructions:

1. Preheat oven to 450°F (230°C). Line a baking sheet with parchment paper.
2. Mix potato flakes, Parmesan, garlic powder, oregano, paprika, salt, and pepper in a shallow dish.
3. Dip each chicken cutlet in beaten eggs, then coat with potato-Parmesan mixture.
4. Place chicken on prepared baking sheet. Drizzle with olive oil.
5. Bake for 15-18 minutes, until golden brown and cooked through.

Prep time: 10 minutes. Cook time: 18 minutes. Total time: 28 minutes. Serves: 4

Total Nutrition (per serving): Calories: 390; Protein: 35g; Carbs: 20g; Fat: 15g.

Description: This Super Crispy Potato-Parmesan Crusted Chicken is a 30-minute miracle for busy weeknights. Using thin cutlets and a higher oven temperature, we've created an incredibly crispy exterior while keeping the chicken juicy inside. It's a healthier alternative to fried chicken that doesn't sacrifice on flavor or texture. Perfect for those who crave comfort food but are short on time!

Easy Tuna Noodle Casserole

Ingredients:

- 8 oz (225g) egg noodles
- 2 cans (5 oz each) tuna in water, drained
- 1 can (10.5 oz) cream of mushroom soup
- 1 cup frozen peas
- 1 cup shredded cheddar cheese
- 1/2 cup milk
- 1/4 cup breadcrumbs
- 1 tbsp butter, melted
- Salt and pepper to taste

Instructions:

1. Preheat oven to 375°F (190°C). Grease a 9x13 inch baking dish.
2. Cook noodles according to package instructions, drain.
3. In a large bowl, mix noodles, tuna, soup, peas, 1/2 cup cheese, milk, salt, and pepper.
4. Transfer mixture to the baking dish. Top with remaining cheese.
5. Mix breadcrumbs with melted butter, sprinkle over the top.
6. Bake for 15-20 minutes until bubbly and golden.

Prep time: 10 minutes. Cook time: 20 minutes. Total time: 30 minutes. Serves: 4

Total Nutrition (per serving): Calories: 350; Protein: 25g; Carbs: 35g; Fat: 12g.

Description: This Easy Tuna Noodle Casserole is a comforting classic that comes together in just 30 minutes. It's perfect for busy weeknights when you need a satisfying meal but don't have much time. Using common pantry staples, this dish offers a balanced mix of protein, carbs, and vegetables. It's a budget-friendly option that's sure to please the whole family.

Quick Skillet Stuffed Bell Peppers

Ingredients:

- 4 bell peppers, tops removed and seeded
- 1 lb lean ground beef
- 1 cup instant rice
- 1 cup water
- 1 can (14.5 oz) diced tomatoes
- 1 tsp Italian seasoning
- 1 cup shredded cheese
- Salt and pepper to taste

Instructions:

1. In a microwave-safe bowl, combine instant rice and 1 cup water. Microwave for 5 minutes, then fluff with a fork.
2. Meanwhile, microwave peppers for 2-3 minutes until slightly softened.
3. In a large skillet, brown beef over medium-high heat, 5 minutes.
4. Stir in cooked rice, half the tomatoes, and seasonings.
5. Stuff peppers with the beef mixture, place in skillet.
6. Pour remaining tomatoes around peppers.
7. Cover, simmer for 10 minutes until peppers are tender.
8. Top with cheese, cover until melted, about 2 minutes.

Prep time: 10 minutes. Cook time: 20 minutes. Total time: 30 minutes. Serves: 4

Total Nutrition (per serving): Calories: 300; Protein: 20g; Carbs: 35g; Fat: 8g.

Description: This Quick Skillet Stuffed Bell Peppers recipe delivers all the flavors of traditional stuffed peppers in just 30 minutes. By pre-softening the peppers and using a skillet method, we've significantly reduced cooking time without sacrificing taste. It's a perfect weeknight dinner that's both satisfying and nutritious.

Strategies for Excellent Dinners

1. Weekly menu planning: • Dedicate 15 minutes on weekends for planning • Consider family schedules and seasonal produce • Alternate protein features and cuisines
2. Smart use of leftovers: • Turn leftover chicken into salads or wraps • Use vegetables in omelets or frittatas • Add yesterday's rice to soups or fried rice
3. Pantry staples for quick dinners: • Canned beans and tomatoes • Frozen vegetables and ready-made dough • Various pasta shapes • Stock cubes and sauces
4. Time-saving cooking techniques: • Use a slow cooker or pressure cooker • Prep vegetables in advance and store in containers • Marinate meat in the morning or the night before

Clever Hacks for Speedy Dinners

1. Efficient use of kitchen appliances: • Use a slow cooker for large batches and stews • Apply an immersion blender for quick pureed soups • Cook in a steamer to preserve nutrients

2. Quick cutting secrets: • Use scissors for fast herb and vegetable chopping • Apply an egg slicer for soft vegetables and fruits • Slice multiple cherry tomatoes at once between two plates

3. Food storage tricks: • Store herbs in jars with water in the fridge for freshness • Freeze fresh herbs in ice cube trays with olive oil • Use vacuum seal bags to extend food shelf life

4. Plating tips: • Use colorful vegetables for visually appealing dishes • Serve dinner on large plates for an impressive presentation • Add fresh herbs before serving for brightness and aroma

5. Family engagement ideas: • Host themed dinner nights (e.g., Mexican or Italian cuisine) • Let kids plan the menu once a week • Create a "build-your-own" taco or burrito station for the whole family

Sweet Treats and Satisfying Bites in
30 Minutes or Less

Welcome to the world of quick and delicious desserts and snacks! In this section, we'll explore how to satisfy your sweet tooth and curb those mid-day cravings without spending hours in the kitchen. Whether you're looking for an after-dinner treat or a pick-me-up between meals, these recipes are designed to be both time-efficient and irresistibly tasty.

Why Quick Desserts and Snacks Matter:
- Instant gratification: Sometimes, you just need a treat, and you need it now.
- Portion control: Smaller, quicker recipes often mean better portion sizes.
- Fresh is best: Many quick desserts use fresh ingredients for maximum flavor.
- Customizable: These recipes are easy to adapt to dietary needs or preferences.
- Fun for the whole family: Get kids involved in these simple, fun recipes.

What to Expect in This Section:
- 10 dessert and snack recipes, each ready in 30 minutes or less
- A mix of sweet and savory options to suit all taste buds
- Ingredients you likely already have in your pantry
- Tips for making ahead and storing your treats
- Ideas for healthier substitutions and variations

Remember, these quick desserts and snacks are perfect for:
- Unexpected guests
- Last-minute potluck contributions
- After-school treats for kids
- Late-night cravings
- Quick energy boosts during a busy day

Let's dive in and discover how easy it can be to whip up something delightful in no time!

Mastering the Art of Speedy Sweets and Snacks

Stock Your Pantry:
* Keep basics like flour, sugar, baking powder, and vanilla on hand
* Stock up on nuts, dried fruits, and chocolate chips
* Have a variety of crackers, pretzels, and popcorn for quick snacks

Embrace No-Bake Options:
* Explore recipes that don't require an oven
* Try refrigerator or freezer desserts for hot days
* Use the microwave for quick mug cakes and melting chocolate

Leverage Your Appliances:
* Use a food processor for quick crusts and batters
* Employ an electric mixer for faster whipping and mixing
* Don't forget your microwave for melting and quick cooking

Prep Ahead:
* Pre-measure dry ingredients and store in labeled containers
* Chop nuts and fruits in advance and keep in the freezer
* Make large batches of snack mixes and store in airtight containers

Smart Substitutions:
* Use Greek yogurt instead of heavy cream for a healthier option
* Swap in whole wheat flour for added nutrition
* Try natural sweeteners like honey or maple syrup instead of sugar

Quick Decorating Tips:
* Use fresh fruit for an instant, beautiful topping
* Sprinkle powdered sugar through a small sieve for a professional look
* Drizzle melted chocolate for an elegant touch

Remember, the key to quick desserts and snacks is simplicity. Focus on quality ingredients, simple techniques, and let the natural flavors shine!

Quick and Easy Chocolate Chip Cookies

Ingredients:

- 2 1/4 cups all-purpose flour
- 1 tsp baking soda
- 1 tsp salt
- 1 cup unsalted butter, softened
- 3/4 cup granulated sugar
- 3/4 cup packed brown sugar
- 2 large eggs
- 1 tsp vanilla extract
- 2 cups semisweet chocolate chips

Instructions:

1. Preheat oven to 375°F (190°C). Line baking sheets with parchment paper.
2. In a medium bowl, whisk together flour, baking soda, and salt. Set aside.
3. In a large bowl, beat butter and both sugars until creamy, about 2 minutes.
4. Beat in eggs one at a time, then stir in vanilla.
5. Gradually mix in the flour mixture. Stir in chocolate chips.
6. Drop rounded tablespoons of dough onto prepared baking sheets.
7. Bake for 9-11 minutes or until golden brown.
8. Cool on baking sheets for 2 minutes, then transfer to wire racks.

Prep time: 10 minutes. Cook time: 11 minutes. Total time: 21 minutes. Serves: 24

Total Nutrition (per cookie): Calories: 160; Protein: 2g; Carbs: 22g; Fat: 8g.

Description: These classic chocolate chip cookies are a staple in American homes. Ready in just over 20 minutes, they're perfect for satisfying sudden sweet cravings or preparing a quick treat for unexpected guests. The recipe yields soft, chewy cookies with crisp edges and gooey chocolate chips. It's an ideal project to involve kids in the kitchen, teaching them basic baking skills while creating delicious memories.

Quick Apple Crumble

Ingredients:
- 4 large apples, cored and chopped (not peeled)
- 1/4 cup granulated sugar
- 1 tsp ground cinnamon
- 1/4 tsp ground nutmeg

For the topping:
- 1 cup quick-cooking oats
- 1/2 cup brown sugar
- 1/4 cup all-purpose flour
- 1/4 cup unsalted butter, melted
- 1/4 tsp salt

Instructions:
1. Preheat oven to 375°F (190°C).
2. In a bowl, mix apples, sugar, cinnamon, and nutmeg. Spread in a 9-inch microwave-safe baking dish.
3. Microwave apple mixture on high for 5 minutes.
4. Meanwhile, in another bowl, combine oats, brown sugar, flour, melted butter, and salt.
5. Sprinkle topping over microwaved apples.
6. Bake for 15-20 minutes until topping is golden and apples are tender.

Prep time: 10 minutes. Cook time: 20 minutes. Total time: 30 minutes. Serves: 6

Total Nutrition (per serving): Calories: 270; Protein: 2g; Carbs: 52g; Fat: 10g.

Description: This quick apple crumble is a comforting dessert that captures the essence of American home baking, ready in just 30 minutes. By using chopped, unpeeled apples and quick-cooking oats, we've streamlined the process without sacrificing flavor. The warm, spiced apples contrast beautifully with the crisp, buttery topping. Serve with a scoop of vanilla ice cream for a classic à la mode experience.

5-Minute Microwave Chocolate Mug Cake

Ingredients:

- 4 tbsp all-purpose flour
- 4 tbsp granulated sugar
- 2 tbsp unsweetened cocoa powder
- 1/4 tsp baking powder
- 1/4 tsp salt
- 1 large egg
- 3 tbsp milk
- 3 tbsp vegetable oil
- 1/2 tsp vanilla extract
- 2 tbsp chocolate chips

Instructions:

1. In a large microwave-safe mug, mix flour, sugar, cocoa powder, baking powder, and salt.
2. Add egg, milk, oil, and vanilla. Whisk until smooth.
3. Stir in chocolate chips.
4. Microwave on high for 1-2 minutes, until cake is cooked through.
5. Let cool for 1 minute before serving.

Prep time: 3 minutes. Cook time: 2 minutes. Total time: 5 minutes. Serves: 1

Total Nutrition (per serving): Calories: 410; Protein: 8g; Carbs: 64g; Fat: 16g.

Description: This 5-minute chocolate mug cake is the ultimate quick dessert for busy Americans. Perfect for late-night cravings or a speedy after-dinner treat, it delivers a warm, gooey chocolate cake with minimal effort and cleanup. The addition of chocolate chips creates pockets of melted chocolate throughout, making each bite a delightful surprise. Serve as is or top with a scoop of vanilla ice cream for an extra indulgent touch.

3-Ingredient Peanut Butter Cookies

Ingredients:
- 1 cup creamy peanut butter
- 3/4 cup granulated sugar
- 1 large egg
- (Optional) 1/4 tsp vanilla extract for enhanced flavor

Instructions:
1. Preheat oven to 350°F (175°C). Line a baking sheet with parchment paper.
2. In a medium bowl, mix peanut butter, sugar, egg, and vanilla (if using) until well combined.
3. Scoop tablespoon-sized balls of dough onto the prepared baking sheet.
4. Use a fork to create a crisscross pattern on each cookie, flattening slightly.
5. Bake for 10-12 minutes, until edges are lightly golden.
6. Allow to cool on the baking sheet for 5 minutes before transferring to a wire rack.

Prep time: 10 minutes. Cook time: 12 minutes. Total time: 22 minutes. Serves: 24 cookies

Total Nutrition (per cookie): Calories: 180; Protein: 4g; Carbs: 18g; Fat: 10g.

Description: These quick and easy flourless peanut butter cookies are a perfect solution for last-minute dessert cravings. With just three main ingredients and less than 30 minutes from start to finish, they're an ideal choice for busy households. The cookies have a rich peanut butter flavor and a unique, tender texture that's slightly different from traditional flour-based cookies. They're naturally gluten-free, making them suitable for those with dietary restrictions.

Note: This recipe uses no flour, which may surprise some bakers. The peanut butter acts as the main binding agent, resulting in a softer, more delicate cookie than traditional recipes. If you prefer a firmer texture, you can add 1/2 cup of all-purpose flour to the mix.

Quick Individual Strawberry Shortcakes

Ingredients:

- 2 cups all-purpose flour
- 1/4 cup granulated sugar
- 1 tablespoon baking powder
- 1/2 teaspoon salt
- 1/3 cup cold unsalted butter, cubed
- 3/4 cup cold milk
- 1 pound fresh strawberries, sliced
- 2 tablespoons sugar (for strawberries)
- 1 cup heavy whipping cream
- 2 tablespoons powdered sugar
- 1/2 teaspoon vanilla extract

Instructions:

1. Preheat oven to 425°F (220°C). Line a baking sheet with parchment paper.
2. In a large bowl, mix flour, sugar, baking powder, and salt.
3. Cut in butter until mixture resembles coarse crumbs.
4. Stir in milk just until moistened. Drop by 1/3 cupfuls onto baking sheet.
5. Bake for 12-15 minutes or until golden brown. Cool slightly.
6. Meanwhile, mix sliced strawberries with 2 tablespoons sugar.
7. Whip cream with powdered sugar and vanilla until stiff peaks form.
8. Split shortcakes; fill with strawberries and whipped cream.

Prep time: 10 minutes. Cook time: 15 minutes. Total time: 25 minutes. Serves: 6

Total Nutrition (per serving): Calories: 310; Protein: 5g; Carbs: 52g; Fat: 11g.

Description: This quick strawberry shortcake is perfect for a speedy yet impressive dessert.

Note: For a quicker version, use store-bought pound cake or biscuits. You can also experiment with other berries or soft fruits like raspberries, blueberries, or peaches.

Quick Caramel Apple Galette

Ingredients:
- 1 sheet pre-made puff pastry, thawed
- 2 large apples, thinly sliced
- 2 tablespoons sugar
- 1 teaspoon cinnamon
- 1/4 teaspoon nutmeg
- 1/4 cup (60 ml) caramel sauce (store-bought or homemade)
- 1 egg, beaten (for egg wash)

Instructions:
1. Preheat oven to 400°F (200°C). Unroll pastry on parchment paper.
2. Mix apples with sugar, cinnamon, and nutmeg.
3. Arrange apples in the center of the pastry, leaving a 2-inch border.
4. Fold pastry edges over apples, creating pleats.
5. Brush edges with beaten egg.
6. Bake for 20-25 minutes until golden brown.
7. Drizzle with caramel sauce before serving.

Prep time: 10 minutes. Cook time: 20 minutes. Total time: 30 minutes. Serves: 4

Total Nutrition (per serving): Calories: 390; Protein: 4g; Carbs: 62g; Fat: 15g.

Description: This quick caramel apple galette combines flaky pastry, juicy apples, and sweet caramel sauce. It's a simple yet impressive dessert, perfect for a fall evening or when you want something special but quick.

Note: Use rough, uneven edges for a rustic look. Serve warm with a scoop of vanilla ice cream for extra indulgence. If caramel sauce is not readily available, you can make a quick version by melting 1/4 cup (50g) of sugar in a pan over medium heat until golden brown, then carefully stirring in 2 tablespoons of heavy cream and 1 tablespoon of butter. Let it cool slightly before using.

Quick Homemade Nachos

Ingredients:
- 1 bag (13 oz) tortilla chips
- 2 cups shredded cheddar cheese
- 1 can (15 oz) black beans, drained and rinsed
- 1 cup diced tomatoes mixed with 2 tablespoons finely chopped onion and 1 tablespoon lime juice
- 1 large avocado, diced
- 1/4 cup sliced pickled peppers or fresh bell peppers (optional)
- 1/4 cup sour cream
- 2 tablespoons chopped fresh cilantro or parsley

Instructions:
1. Preheat oven to 350°F (175°C).
2. Spread tortilla chips on a large, oven-safe platter or baking sheet.
3. Sprinkle cheese and black beans over chips.
4. Bake for 10-15 minutes, until cheese is melted and bubbly.
5. Remove from oven and immediately top with tomato mixture, avocado, peppers, sour cream, and cilantro or parsley.
6. Serve hot.

Prep time: 5 minutes. Cook time: 15 minutes. Total time: 20 minutes. Serves: 4-6

Total Nutrition (per serving): Calories: 320; Protein: 12g; Carbs: 45g; Fat: 15g.

Description: These quick homemade nachos are perfect for game day, movie night, or anytime you need a satisfying snack in a hurry. Loaded with melty cheese, beans, and fresh toppings, they offer a balance of flavors and textures that's hard to resist.

Note: Feel free to customize with additional toppings like cooked ground beef, shredded chicken, or extra vegetables. For a healthier version, use baked tortilla chips and low-fat cheese.

Quick Buffalo Chicken Wings

Ingredients:
- 1 lb chicken wings, split at joints, tips discarded
- 1 tablespoon vegetable oil
- 1/2 teaspoon salt
- 1/4 teaspoon black pepper
- 1/3 cup hot sauce (like Frank's RedHot)
- 2 tablespoons unsalted butter, melted
- 1 teaspoon white vinegar
- 1/4 teaspoon garlic powder
- Celery sticks and blue cheese or ranch dressing, for serving

Instructions:
1. Preheat oven to 450°F (230°C). Line a baking sheet with aluminum foil.
2. In a bowl, toss wings with oil, salt, and pepper.
3. Arrange wings on the baking sheet in a single layer.
4. Bake for 20-25 minutes, turning once halfway through, until crispy and cooked through.
5. Meanwhile, in a large bowl, whisk together hot sauce, melted butter, vinegar, and garlic powder.
6. When wings are done, toss them in the sauce mixture until well coated.
7. Serve immediately with celery sticks and dressing on the side.

Prep time: 5 minutes. Cook time: 25 minutes. Total time: 30 minutes. Serves: 2-3

Total Nutrition (per serving): Calories: 350; Protein: 25g; Carbs: 5g; Fat: 25g.

Description: These quick Buffalo chicken wings deliver the classic spicy, tangy flavor in just 30 minutes. Perfect for game day or a fast snack, they offer all the taste of traditional wings with a fraction of the cooking time.

Note: For a milder version, use less hot sauce and more butter. You can also experiment with different sauces like BBQ or honey garlic for variety.

Quick Loaded Potato Skins

Ingredients:

- 4 medium russet potatoes
- 2 tablespoons olive oil
- 1/2 teaspoon salt
- 1/4 teaspoon black pepper
- 1 cup shredded cheddar cheese
- 4 slices bacon, cooked and crumbled
- 2 green onions, thinly sliced
- 1/4 cup sour cream

Instructions:

1. Preheat oven to 400°F (200°C).
2. Scrub potatoes and prick with a fork. Microwave on high for 5-7 minutes until tender.
3. Cut potatoes in half lengthwise; scoop out pulp, leaving a 1/4-inch shell.
4. Brush both sides of potato skins with oil; sprinkle with salt and pepper.
5. Place on a baking sheet and bake for 10 minutes.
6. Flip skins over and bake for another 5 minutes until crispy.
7. Fill with cheese and bacon; bake for 2-3 minutes until cheese melts.
8. Top with green onions and serve with sour cream.

Prep time: 10 minutes. Cook time: 20 minutes. Total time: 30 minutes. Serves: 4

Total Nutrition (per serving): Calories: 280; Protein: 8g; Carbs: 35g; Fat: 12g.

Description: These quick loaded potato skins are a classic American appetizer, perfect for game day or as a satisfying snack. Crispy on the outside, cheesy and bacon-filled on the inside, they're sure to be a crowd-pleaser.

Note: For a vegetarian version, omit the bacon and add extra vegetables like diced bell peppers or jalapeños.

Quick Spinach and Artichoke Dip

Ingredients:

- 1 (14 oz) can artichoke hearts, drained and chopped
- 1 (10 oz) package frozen chopped spinach, thawed and drained
- 8 oz cream cheese (like Philadelphia), softened
- 1/4 cup mayonnaise
- 1/4 cup grated Parmesan cheese
- 1/4 cup shredded mozzarella cheese
- 2 cloves garlic, minced
- 1/4 teaspoon salt
- 1/4 teaspoon black pepper
- Tortilla chips or sliced baguette for serving

Instructions:

1. Preheat oven to 375°F (190°C).
2. In a large bowl, mix all ingredients (except chips/bread) until well combined.
3. Transfer mixture to a 1-quart baking dish.
4. Bake for 20 minutes until hot and bubbly.
5. Serve immediately with tortilla chips or sliced baguette.

Prep time: 10 minutes. Cook time: 20 minutes. Total time: 30 minutes. Serves: 6-8

Total Nutrition (per serving): Calories: 250; Protein: 10g; Carbs: 10g; Fat: 20g.

Description: This quick spinach and artichoke dip is a crowd-pleasing appetizer that comes together in just 30 minutes. Creamy, cheesy, and packed with vegetables, it's perfect for parties or as a indulgent snack.

Note: For a lighter version, use low-fat cream cheese and Greek yogurt instead of mayonnaise. You can also add diced jalapeños for a spicy kick.

Tricks for Swift Sweets and Satisfying Bites

- Pantry Staples:
    - Keep nuts, dried fruits, chocolate chips, premade crusts
    - Keep variety of cookies and crackers for quick dessert bases
- Time-Saving Techniques:
    - Use microwave for melting; opt for no-bake recipes
    - Prep ingredients in advance
- Healthy Swaps:
    - Greek yogurt for cream; mashed fruit for sugar
    - Air-popped popcorn for lighter snacks
- Presentation Hacks:
    - Use mason jars or shot glasses for individual servings
    - Garnish with powdered sugar or cocoa

Speedy Sweet and Savory Treats

- 5-Minute Fruit Kebabs:
    - Thread seasonal fruits on skewers
    - Drizzle with honey or chocolate for extra flavor
- Microwave Chocolate-Dipped Strawberries:
    - Melt chocolate in microwave, dip strawberries
    - Let set in refrigerator for quick indulgence
- No-Bake Yogurt Parfait:
    - Layer Greek yogurt, granola, and berries in a glass
    - Customize with favorite fruits and nuts
- Custom Trail Mix:
    - Combine preferred nuts, seeds, and dried fruits
    - Add dark chocolate chips for a sweet touch
- Energy Balls:
    - Blend dates, nuts, and oats in food processor
    - Roll into balls for portable, nutritious snacks

Index

Shrimp
Lemon Garlic Pasta, 54
Lemon Garlic Salad, 64
Smoothies
Green Tea, 6
Tropical Sunrise, 18
Soups
Noodle, 42
Tomato, 40
Spinach
Artichoke Dip, 108
Egg Muffins, 10
Breakfast Quesadilla, 24
Strawberry Shortcakes, 98
T
Teriyaki Chicken, 56
Toast
Avocado, 26
Ricotta, 12
Tomato Soup, 40
Turkey
Breakfast Quesadilla, 24
Skillet, 72
Tuna
Avocado Power Bowl, 38
Noodle Casserole, 82
V
Vegetarian Dishes, 6, 8, 18, 22, 34, 44, 90, 92, 94, 96, 98, 108
W
Wings, Buffalo Chicken, 104
Wraps, Chicken, 36

Nutritional Information Note

Please note that the nutritional values provided for each recipe are approximate and can vary depending on the specific brands and quantities of ingredients used. While these values have been carefully calculated, they are intended to serve as a general guide. For the most accurate nutritional information, we recommend using a food nutrition calculator with the exact products you use.

Conclusion

Dear Reader,

As we come to the end of this culinary journey, I hope that "Quick and Healthy 30 Minute Recipes for Busy People" has inspired you to embrace the joy of cooking, even on your busiest days. Remember, eating healthily doesn't have to be time-consuming or complicated. With the recipes and tips in this book, you now have the tools to create delicious, nutritious meals in 30 minutes or less.

I encourage you to experiment with these recipes, make them your own, and most importantly, enjoy the process. Cooking is not just about nourishing our bodies; it's about creating moments of joy and connection in our daily lives.

For those interested in exploring more specialized diets, keep an eye out for my upcoming books on anti-inflammatory, keto, and vegetarian cuisines.

Thank you for allowing me to be a part of your cooking journey. Here's to many more delicious, healthy, and quick meals in your future!

Bon appétit!

Emily Harper

Acknowledgments

I would like to express my heartfelt gratitude to:
- My grandmother, whose passion for cooking sparked my culinary journey
- My family and friends, for their unwavering support and taste-testing
- You, the reader, for choosing to prioritize your health and well-being

Your support makes it possible for me to continue sharing my love for healthy, quick cooking with the world.

Made in the USA
Monee, IL
14 January 2025